THE CRY OF THE BLIND

A CALL TO THE CHURCH TO EVANGELIZE THE LOST

WESLEY V. KNIGHT

GOD'S LIFE
PUBLISHING

THE CRY OF THE BLIND by Wesley V. Knight

Published by God's Life Publishing

5369 Edgewater Dr. Ewa Beach, Hawaii 96706
Email: godlife@aol.com   www.godslifepublishing.org

This book or parts thereof may not be reproduced in any form, stored in a retrieval system, or transmitted in any form by any means—electronic, mechanical, photocopy, recording, or otherwise for commercial gain or profit—without prior written permission of the publisher. The use of short quotations or occasional page copying for personal or group study is permitted and encourage.
Unless otherwise identified, Scripture quotations are from the King James Version of the Bible.

Cover design by God's Life Publishing

Copyright ©2018 by Wesley V. Knight
All rights reserved

International Standard Book Number: 978-0-9916263-6-6
E-book ISBN: 978-0-9916263-7-3
Printed in the United States of America

Dedication

I would like to dedicate this book to my Lord and Savior Jesus Christ. This work would not have been possible without his guidance and help. Also, to my wife, Adriene Knight, I say thank you for all of your support and love over these 28 years. To my daughters, Camille, Christina, and Kenyetta and my grandson Jamel, thank you for the sacrifices that you have made so that I am able to be and still become what God desires. To Bishop Michael A. Blue and Pastor Malinda J. Blue, thank you for all of your prayers, support and encouragement throughout this project. To the New Creation Christian Church, the Christian Covenant Fellowship of Ministries, and the New York City CCFM Leadership Alliance, thank you for your unwavering dedication and encouragement throughout the years. To the rest of my family, thank you for all of your prayers and support. In memory of my mother, Evangelist Barbara Knight, I am thankful for the things I've learned from her life of always seeking to hear and respond to the cry of the blind.

TABLE OF CONTENTS

Introduction		1
Chapter 1 -	The Cry of the Blind	5
Chapter 2-	The Blind Among Us	11
Chapter 3 -	The Church Then & The Church Now	17
Chapter 4 -	The Proper Role Of The Church	29
Chapter 5 -	Empty Vessels	37
Chapter 6 -	Be Filled With The Spirit	43
Chapter 7 -	Return To The Mission	49
Chapter 8 -	I Am Not Ashamed Of The Gospel	55
Chapter 9 -	Search For The Lost	59
Chapter 10 -	Use The Name Of Jesus	63
Chapter 11 -	Evangelize The Blind	69
Conclusion -		73
About the Author		75
Contact the Author		77
Additional Resources Available from Bishop Knight		79

INTRODUCTION

America is currently in the midst of a social, economic and spiritual downturn. The spiritual condition of individuals that makeup the Body of Christ is so dismal that the prophet Jeremiah coined the phrase that we are "at ease in Zion". We've become so relaxed that we are blind to the needs of our fellowman and the command of our Savior to "Go ye therefore, and teach all nations, baptizing them in the name of the Father, and of the Son, and of the Holy Ghost" (Matthew 28:19). Only when we return to addressing the spiritual condition of every citizen will we see a positive change in our nation.

Though we see people around us being squeezed out of jobs because of their age or just because they make too much money (two more people could be hired with their salary), we still fail to see the need. Hope of the American dream is all but gone. Many have questions and no answer. Some are asking, who can afford to pay a mortgage and property taxes for a home?

CRY OF THE BLIND

Children are seen as a liability and not as a gift from God. Families are breaking up. The divorce rate is rising and some individuals are not even bothering to get married at all. Every abomination that scripture speaks against is now being flaunted as the new normal. There is no privacy, decency or moral code even in public bathrooms. Many sinners including professing Christians are turning to drugs, alcohol, and crime to ease the pain of their current circumstances.

In the Old Testament (Jeremiah 8:18-22) the prophet Jeremiah laments for Judah because of the cry that is coming from the depths of their anguished, broken and distraught heart. They have trusted in themselves and their idols rather than turning to the living God. They expected God to intervene even though they turned their back on Him. They loved sin more than the precepts of God. Many are asking the same question that was uttered by Jeremiah.

"Is there no balm in Gilead; is there no physician there? why then is not the health of the daughter of my people recovered" (Jeremiah 8:22).

Jeremiah knew the mercy of God and wept because the people had gone so far from God they were not saved or recovered from their sin sickness. Likewise, it breaks my heart because many people are crying in their distresses, but those who know the Great physician and the Holy Spirit are not leading the people to the spiritual hospital for health and healing. Truly the hour is come that we like the early disciples must go out into the highways and hedges and fulfill Jesus

Introduction

mission to seek and save the lost. Though we may be in the eleventh hour, there is still time to open our deaf ears, hear the cry of the blind and launch a rescue mission. I believe the finest hour of the church is on the horizon when we make an all out effort to gather the harvest for the Lord. The fields are white and are waiting for you and I to do the work of the evangelist.

CRY OF THE BLIND

CHAPTER 1

The Cry Of the Blind

We will use a story of a blind man in scripture to begin our examination of identifying those in our midst that are blind and what our response ought to be. The story of Blind Bartimaeus is so significant it is recorded in three Gospel accounts (Luke 18:35-43), (Mark 10:46-52) and (Matthew 20:29-34). For our purposes we will use Luke's recording.

> *"And it came to pass, that as he was come nigh unto Jericho, a certain blind man sat by the way side begging" (Luke 18:35):*

Luke tells us that Jericho was the location where this event takes place.

CRY OF THE BLIND

He also begins to paint a picture for us about a specific blind man. Let us seek to get an understanding of what it means to say a person is blind. There are a number of ways to define and examine what blindness is. The Merrian-Webster dictionary defines the blind as those who are sightless, unable or unwilling to discern or judge. The blind is also those who have no regard to rational discrimination, guidance, or restriction.

We can also define blindness from a medical perspective. It would simply be defined as a loss of useful sight. It can be temporary or permanent. Damage to any portion of the eye, the optic nerve, or the area of the brain responsible for vision can lead to blindness. There are three categories of blindness (sudden, gradual and chronic) that has been observed in scripture. When flies, dirt, dust, and glare get into the eyes it can result in sudden blindness. Gradual blindness is caused by old age, and chronic blindness is seen in individuals who were born blind.

Spiritual blindness is far more destructive than any of the other conditions that result in blindness. The spiritual blind do not see Jesus Christ and therefore they do not see their creator God. These individuals choose not to accept the teachings of Christ and His authority in their lives. They have an unbelieving heart, are lost in their sin, and have a blockage when it comes to believing that things can be better with the Lord's help.

Let us come along side Jesus as he approaches a blind

The Cry Of The Blind

beggar near Jericho, known as "Blind Bartimaeus".

He was one of the many beggars who lined the roads of Jericho in the days of Jesus. As Jesus left Jericho, there was a great uproar from the multitude that followed him. Though Bartimaeus had no ability to see anyone, he heard the commotion, which told him that something was happening.

"And hearing the multitude pass by, he asked what it meant. And they told him, that Jesus of Nazareth passeth by (Luke 18:36-37).

He wanted to know what was going on because he heard the noise. Today, many people are not inquiring about what is happening in the Church because we are not making enough noise. The blind people in the world are not showing an interest in the Church or what the Church represents simply because the Church is too quiet about the love and power of Jesus to transform their lives.

In this story recorded by Luke the physician, the sighted told Blind Bartimaeus the noise (commotion) meant that Jesus of Nazareth was passing by. Luke further records that the blind beggar cried out saying,

> *"Jesus, thou son of David, have mercy on me. And they which went before rebuked him, that he should hold his peace: but he cried so much the more, Thou son of David, have mercy on me" (Luke 18:38-39).*

His actions give us an indication that he was acquainted with the ministry of Jesus, or at least he had heard about the ministry of Jesus. At any rate, it is clear that he had an agenda to get Jesus's attention. He would not have cried out to Jesus if he did not believe Jesus could help him. Like Bartimaeus, when we seek help, we seek it from those we believe can provide the type of aid or support we need.

Since the physical circumstances of Bartimaeus blindness it is not recorded, we do not know whether he was born blind or had an accident. All three Gospels make it clear that Bartimaeus was physically blind. Luke indicates that he had to be lead by the hand to Jesus because he could not see.

Jesus used this situation as another teaching moment for his disciples as he was on the way to the cross. Jesus demonstrated the teaching in the Old Testament that taught how we are supposed to treat the blind. The manner in which he dealt with Blind Bartimaeus was designed to bring John 3:16 to life. Love cared for the blind, love had compassion for the cry of the blind, love passed no judgment on the reason why they were blind and ultimately love gives sight to the blind.

"Cursed is he that maketh the blind to wander out of the way" (Deuteronomy 27:18).

"Thou shalt not curse the deaf, nor put a stumblingblock before the blind, but shalt fear thy God: I am the Lord" (Leviticus 19:14).

"The Lord openeth the eyes of the blind: the Lord raiseth them that are bowed down: the Lord loveth the righteous" (Psalm 146:8).

The Cry Of The Blind

"And in that day shall the deaf hear the words of the book, and the eyes of the blind shall see out of obscurity, and out of darkness" (Isaiah 29:18).

"I the Lord has called thee in righteousness, ...To open the blind eyes, to bring out the prisoners from the prison, and them that sit in darkness out of the prison house" (Isaiah 42:6-7).

"And I will bring the blind by a way that they knew not; I will lead them in paths that they have not known: I will make darkness light before them, and crooked things straight. These things will I do unto them, and not forsake them" (Isaiah 42:16).

Jesus action was intended to teach the disciples by word and deed what would be required of them in responding to the cry of the blind. Likewise we who are disciples of Christ, can imitate Jesus example by taking time to minister to those who are crying out for help. Jesus made it clear on every occasion that it was his mission to respond to the needs of the people. When John asked, "Art thou he that should come or do we look for another?" (Matthew 11:3). Jesus answered and said unto them, "Go and shew John again those things which ye do hear and see: The blind receive their sight, and the lame walk, the lepers are cleansed, and the deaf hear, the dead are raised up, and the poor have the gospel preached to them. And blessed is he, whosoever shall not be offended in me" (Matthew 11:4-6). The first group of people Jesus referred to, as proof that he was Messiah was the blind. Hundreds of years prior, the Old Testament prophet Isaiah prophesy what the disciples had just witnessed when he said,

> *"And in that day shall the deaf hear the words of the book, and the eyes of the blind shall see out of obscurity, and out of darkness. The meek also shall increase their joy in the Lord, and the poor among men shall rejoice in the Holy One of Israel"* (Isaiah 29:18-19).

Isaiah was clearly referring to Jesus when he spoke of the "Holy One" of Israel. The Apostle Luke in the New Testament used a similar title "Holy Thing" to refer to Christ. Upon the announcement of the birth of Christ, he writes,

> *"And the angel answered and said unto her, The Holy Ghost shall come upon thee, and the power of the Highest shall overshadow thee: therefore also that holy thing which shall be born of thee shall be called the Son of God"* (Luke 1:35).

Again and again we see the mission of Christ. It was for this reason that the Son of God was manifested to heal all manner of blindness and sickness.

CHAPTER 2

The Blind Among Us

Today, there is such a great cry of the blind around us and yet many of us are dull of hearing. Even, the religious leaders in our story about Blind Bartimaeus were dull of hearing and did not hear his cry. Luke reveals that sentiment in the following verses of scripture. *"And he cried, saying, Jesus, thou son of David, have mercy on me. And they which went before rebuked him, that he should hold his peace: but he cried so much the more, Thou son of David, have mercy on me"* (Luke 18:38-39). Even though these religious leaders rebuked Bartimaeus, it did not deter him in the least from crying out to Jesus. As a matter of fact, it propelled him to cry out the more to Jesus.

CRY OF THE BLIND

Many of our religious leaders are no different concerning the cry of the blind amongst us. The statistics of gang violence from coast to coast speaks of young people trying to identify in a world of cruelty often by love ones who have abused them. Some are often products of living in homes or foster homes with drug-addicted and sexually deviant caretakers. Many of them turn to the streets for a sense of belonging and for love through some resemblance of a family structure. This leads to struggles with others who are in the same predicament. Again, they are groping in the dark for an answer and yet are coming up short.

Some of the better-known gangs are almost household names. Most of us have heard of those gangs. The gang ring has become more of a family affair than it was in previous times. The New York Daily News headline for June 15, 2008 is titled, *"How Crips, Bloods & Latin Kings "baptize" kids-Baby Gangstas"*. The article explains how one generation of gang bangers are now training their offspring to follow in their footsteps. They even have ceremonies like unto baby christening where they dedicate their children into the gangs. The whole family is now involved in maintaining this life style. These are clearly blind individuals who have no regard to rational guidance or restriction imposed by the laws of God or society.

Others who are crying today are our teenage girls. The current trends suggest that there are more teenagers becoming pregnant than 10 years ago. In the old days, if a young girl got pregnant out of wedlock, her family sent her away privately to another part of the family out of town until she had the baby. Today, it is socially acceptable to have a child out of wedlock. It is a pattern that repeats itself in families who now believe it is all right to have a baby and not be married. These practices are causing our country to deal with an increase of unwanted pregnancies, sexually transmitted diseases (STDs) and a demand for abortions.

Another cry of the blind is the dropout rate in America. It is believed that more than one million students drop out of high school every year. This is staggering in a land of great possibility, where hopes and dreams are realized every day. As a result, many of these youths do not have the necessary skills to succeed in the workplace. This coupled with their troubled home life creates an almost perfect formula for failure. Even these young people need someone to come alongside of him or her to help them to see. Jesus was willing to come alongside of Blind Bartimaeus to help him to see.

> *"And Jesus stood, and commanded him to be brought unto him: and when he was come near, he asked him, Saying, What wilt thou that I shall do unto thee? And he said, Lord, that I may receive my sight. And Jesus said unto him, Receive thy sight: thy faith hath saved thee. And immediately he received his sight, and followed him, glorifying God: and all the people, when they saw it, gave praise unto God" (Luke 18:40-43).*

This blind beggar is finally vindicated and rewarded when

CRY OF THE BLIND

Jesus stopped and ordered those around him to bring him forward. It is quite astonishing that these sighted persons would actually try to stand in the way of someone who needed what they already had. The Bible says this is a faithful saying and worthy of all acceptance that Jesus came and died for sinners. Although Blind Bartimaeus was in close proximity to Jesus, he still needed someone to guide him to the voice that he now heard.

In the Book of the Acts chapter nine, we gain insight on a blind individual who needed guidance to see. The Apostle Luke shares how the Lord encountered Saul of Tarsus on the road to Damascus.

> *"And as he journeyed, he came near Damascus: and suddenly there shined round about him a light from heaven: And he fell to the earth, and heard a voice saying unto him, Saul, Saul, why persecutes thou me? ...And Saul arose from the earth; and when his eyes were opened, he saw no man: but they led him by the hand, and brought him into Damascus. And he was three days without sight, and neither did eat nor drink"* (Acts 9:3-9).

The presence of the light of Christ blinded him. As a result, he needed to be guided into the city to get further instructions from a man of God. Saul's blindness would be considered sudden blindness caused by the Lord himself. The scripture goes on to reveal to us,

> *"And there was a certain disciple at Damascus, named*

Ananias; and to him said the Lord in a vision, Ananias. And he said, Behold, I am here Lord. ...And Ananias went his way, and entered into the house; and putting his hand on him said, Brother Saul, the Lord, even Jesus, that appeared unto thee in the way as thou camest, hath sent me, that thou mightiest receive thy sight, and be filled with the Holy Ghost. And immediately there fell from his eyes as it had been scales: and he received sight forthwith, and arose, and was baptized" (Acts 9:10-18).

Everyone needs someone to help him or her fulfill his or her purpose no matter what the reason for his or her blindness. Maybe you are called be like Ananias. Don't be like him and initially resist being obedient to the voice of God. Because some blind gang banger, sexually active teenage girl, high school dropout and many other blind individuals need you to be an obedient Ananias in their life.

CRY OF THE BLIND

CHAPTER 3

The Church Then and The Church Now

Over the years, the church of Jesus Christ has experienced all kinds of triumphs and failures. It began with the awesome move of Holy Spirit in the Book of Acts with all manner of healing and deliverance. It then continued through the dark ages with persecution from city to city. In more recent times, revival outpourings have filled believers in various places throughout the nation. Not that much has changed since the days of Blind Bartimaeus. When challenges arose in the church it was not the world that created the biggest problem; it was the religious people in the church. There are still religious individuals who have a form of godliness without faith or confidence in the power of Jesus Christ. In spite of these wayward ones, the mission of the church has not changed. It is still to seek, save the lost and the blind.

The Glorious Past Of The Church

We can learn many things about what God intended for his church through Moses the first pastor in the church in the wilderness. The church was always the place that the enslaved, the hungry, the thirst and the blind could go and receive sustenance. Even if God had to use his servant to speak to rocks to quench the thirst of the people, their needs were always met. It was through this church in the wilderness that governments, laws, economics and even fashion were put in place that we still mimic today. Dietary rules and regulations came out of God's church for all of society to benefit. The church was instrumental in shaping and defining the society that they were commanded to lead into the promise land.

In the book, *"What If Jesus Had Never Been Born? The Positive Impact of Christianity in History,"* Dr. James D. Kennedy and Jerry Newcombe imply that society would not have all the programs that aid our daily living, or the liberties of life, health, the pursuit of happiness and peace that we so often neglect. Many fundamental agencies and services that we now have came out of God impressing on the heart of men his mercy and compassion. Since man is a pattern of his creator, church leaders have imitated their God by their acts of benevolence towards others in establishing various organizations.

The synagogue/church was the primary place that individuals could go to learn to read and study God's word. It was a serious matter to the Jewish people that they were to teach their children the sacred scriptures. As time would progress, early church leaders recognized that all children should learn to read, thus Sunday schools were developed. Great centers of learning public and private education came into existence to nurture the minds of many young children. Great advances were made in astronomy, science, travel and medicine all because of the influence of the church.

One might look at the pool of Bethesda (See John 5:1-9) as a type of hospital that the sick gathered believing that they could be healed. Hence, local hospitals, hospice care, convalescent homes and nursing homes came out of the recognition of God's servant to care for the need of the weak, sick and infirmed members of society.

The actions of the Apostle Paul and Barnabas when they gathered resources to alleviate the famine in Judea were acts that would become a forerunner of ministries like the Salvation Army, the Red Cross, Samaritan's Purse and the

Goodwill organization. These and similar institutions come to the aid of those in hurricanes, tornadoes, fires, typhoons and other so called natural disaster. They supply basic needs of clothing, medicine, water, food and even transportation all in an effort to share the Good News.

The church was also instrumental in preserving marriage and family by condemning the practices of child sacrifices, homosexuality, bestiality, polygamy, other sexual perversions, and slavery. These destructive practices caused disease, heartache, broken homes, immoral lifestyle, depression and other psychiatric maladies.

Jesus challenged hypocrisy among so called religious leaders who allowed the moneychangers in the temple. The early church leaders followed Jesus footsteps and confronted wickedness wherever it was found. Stephen preached Christ in the midst of angry sinners who stoned him to death because they refused to believe that Jesus Christ was the Son of God. The Apostle Paul was mocked when he challenged the idolatry of the Athenians who worshiped gods made by hands (See Acts 17). Many other disciples suffered physically when they were beaten with many stripes for preaching the truth and healing many who were afflicted by devils. Not only did the disciples turn the world upside down for Christ, others followed in their footstep and made radical changes in society for Christ. Martin Luther a priest and theologian was not willing to go along to get along with the teaching of the Catholic church on "indulgence" (a way to reduce the amount of punishment one has to undergo for sins by paying money to the Catholic church). As a result, he nailed his Ninety-Five Theses on the door of All Saints Church in Wittenberg, Germany in 1517, and sparked the Protestant Reformation. So great were his convictions that *"salvation is by Christ alone through faith alone"*, that he was willing to be excommunicated from the Roman Catholic Church.

The Current Church

"For we wrestle not against flesh and blood, but against principalities, against powers, against the rulers of the darkness of this world, against spiritual wickedness in high places" (Ephesians 6:12).

The church today has similar challenges like the early church in The Book of Acts. The Devil has not stopped his all out attack on the Church of the Lord Jesus Christ. He has not changed; he has only adjusted his tactics. Professing Christians have changed their response to the Devil's attacks. The early church took the fight to the Devil when they were confronted in preaching the Gospel, accused of stirring up strife, beaten, jailed, and hunted like deer. They did not tone it down, get a lawyer, and change their position on what constituted sin, or shut their mouths. They called on Jesus, submitted to the leading of Holy Spirit, and were willing to suffer persecution so that men would see their good works and glorify the Father. The early church focused on souls being saved.

Today's church is more focused on having things (megachurch, multiple locations, the latest technological gadgets, social media, entertainers who call themselves worshippers, mansions and private airplanes). When people gather into the House of God today, it should not be just a social gathering. They should be coming to hear what the Lord would speak through the preacher. This behavior of being consumed with their own needs hinders the church from fulfilling its' mission. Let us examine four areas that decrease the church's ability to hear the cry of the blind.

Indifference

Sadly, as Bartimaeus reaches for Jesus, those in close proximity of him rebuked the blind man and told him to be quiet. Many times, people in the church who are territorial send those who come to hear the preacher away. Their behavior hinders those who are crying out for help. They are indifferent (having no particular interest or sympathy). The scripture does not give us an explanation of the disciples reasoning. The learned men that were in close proximity to the Messiah did not have any interest in his message or purpose. Many were just watching the show. We further observe the indifference of the religious people in some of the parables Jesus shared. This includes the parable of the little children that came to Jesus (See Matthew 19:13), the feeding of the five thousand (See Mark 6:34-37) and the Canaanite woman with the daughter who was vexed with a devil (See Matthew 15:22-28).

In each instance Jesus was told to *"send them away"*. These disciples kept the children, the spiritual thirsty, and those with physical needs away from Jesus by judging them, limiting their time near Jesus, and imposing their own criteria of worthiness on the people instead of simply inviting them to come and receive what Jesus was offering. The disciples forgot that Jesus came into the world because; he heard the cry of his creation. Likewise many in the Body of Christ, forget that the local pastor is serving because of two major reasons. He or she has been anointed by Jesus to minister the word and he or she is responding to the cry of the blind.

Political Correctness

The political climate in some instances has been allowed to override the voice of the pastors. Many church leaders have been deceived by the devil through the media to embrace the lie that the church should not be involved in politics. In the early 1960's, the idea of a separation between the state and the church was revived. Before that time church leaders openly and publicly campaigned for various governmental candidates, preached against the platform of candidates, and used the Bible to demonstrate the qualities that should be looked for in a candidate. Today, many church leaders are afraid to lose their tax-exempt status so they close their eyes rather than cry out against sin. Political correctness has permeated into many areas when it comes to addressing homosexuality, gay marriage, abortion, euthanasia, human trafficking, child pornography and a whole slew of unmentionables.

Lack of Love

Jesus was fully aware of these times when he shared with the disciples that *"the love of many shall wax cold" (See Matthew 24:12)*. Let us examine a portion of scripture to demonstrate how our love has and is currently waxing cold and thereby dulling our ears from hearing the cry of the blind.

> *"And Jesus, when he came out, saw much people, and was moved with compassion toward them, because they were as sheep not having a shepherd: and he began to teach them many things. And when the day was now far spent, his disciples came unto him, and said, This is a desert place, and now the time is far passed: Send them away, that they may go into the country round about, and into the villages, and buy themselves bread: for they have nothing to eat. He answered and said unto them, Give ye them to eat" (Mark 6:34-37a).*

Though the disciples were tired after a long evangelistic campaign, their uncaring, unfeeling and disregard for the people was not shared by Jesus. The disciples demanded

Jesus to send the multitude away to find something to eat. Jesus ignored the disciple's complaint and commanded them to feed the people. Jesus took many things into consideration in rendering compassion on the people. The three areas that Jesus took into account concerning the people were that they had come from far distances to hear the word, they may not have had any money to purchase bread and evening was approaching. Even in Jesus presence, the disciple's love had clearly waxed cold. Jesus was not and is not interested in man's soul only. He was and is interested in all that pertains to mankind. The wonderful thing about the ministry of Christ is that it works for the whole man.

We can often look around us and see current examples of how Christians have little regard for the struggle of others. In many instances when we see a brother in need, we respond the same as the disciples. Some feel it is someone else responsibility to meet the need and others are too tired from their non-evangelistic schedule to do any evangelism. As ambassadors of Christ, the church is the voice, hands and heart of God. Part of the great success of the church recorded in The Acts of the Apostles was their continual demonstration of genuine love for the people. It was this love that caused them to hear and respond to the cry of the blind.

Love of Money

We live in an age where the love of money dominates many believers. We demonstrate this by our pursuit of promotions on the job, making a fashion statement, home and car ownership as well as owning high tech equipment. These things have blinded many from seeing the needs of others. The love of money has created a selfish mindset among confessing Christians. Some are so possessed with the need for more money that they find it impossible to worship God with their tithes and a worthy offering. As they become more focused on their pursuit of money, they plant less and less into the work of the kingdom and are often the ones who are the first to complain that all the church wants is money. The early disciples cared not for their own wealth, they were willing to joyfully sell their homes and give up personal belongs so that others would have a reasonable measure of comfort. More and more so called Christians are like Ananias and Sapphira willing to lie to the Holy Ghost in order not to fulfill performing their own promises to financially bless God's house (see Acts 5:1-11).

The above listed challenges are not the only ones facing the modern church. The struggle with indifference, political correctness, lack of love and the love of money cripples the church from doing the rudimentary works of Christ. Sometimes the leaders of the church are silent when they ought to lead the way. Even as the disciples declared, ***"we ought to obey God more than man"***, the leaders of our day ought to obey God without wavering. The pastor is oftentimes torn between those members who have been "in the way" and don't want to relinquish their space to those who need that very first encounter with Jesus. Modern day Scribes and Pharisees, still accuse pastors who imitate Jesus of associating with sinners. Jesus understood that the people who needed to be saved and healed had small voices that could not be heard from a far distance. Jesus being the chief shepherd/pastor demonstrates how to listen and respond to the faint cries of the needy in the fourth chapter of the gospel of John. The Apostle John wrote, **"And he (Jesus) must needs go through Samaria"** (see John 4:1-30). There was a sinner in Samaria who was sin sick and calling for help. The religious people were deaf to her whispering voice. Jesus heard the cry and responded. It was not the healthy people who need a physician but this woman who had been married five times and was now living with a man who was not her husband.

Jesus continually reached out to the blind. He was not afraid to be seen among the likes of Zacchaeus, the shady tax collector (see Luke 19:1-10). He came in contact with this chief tax collector with a plan to offer him salvation. Even in Jesus' final moments on the earth, while hanging on the cross, he took an opportunity to evangelize the lost. He heard the cry of the "blind" thief hanging next to him, who said, **"Remember me when thou comest into thy kingdom"** (Luke 23:42-43). In his hour of agony and what looked like defeat, he took time to show love and compassion to a man who was guilty of taking advantage of others. Again, the Intercessor was not in the pulpit but was out in the field for all men to see and hear the gospel preached in word, deed and life.

CRY OF THE BLIND

Likewise, the members of God's church must roll up their sleeves and do the work of the evangelist while following the example of Jesus Christ. The blind matter to Christ and they must matter to us also.

Chapter 4

The Proper Role Of The Church

"Go ye therefore, and teach all nations, baptizing them in the name of the Father, and of the Son, and of the Holy Ghost: Teaching them to observe all things whatsoever I have commanded you: and, lo, I am with you alway, even unto the end of the world. Amen" (Matthew 28:19).

In Matthew 28:19 the KJV translates *"teach"* in Strong's Concordance G3100 to be a disciple of one, to follow his precepts and instructions with the goal of making a disciple by teaching and instructing someone else. This underlying idea from Jesus is the very foundation that the Church must build upon. The role of the church is to nurture disciples through teaching so that one-day these individuals will be equipped to disciple others.

In Acts 1:1, Luke the physician powerfully states that Jesus ministry was to do and to teach. In other words Jesus demonstrated, carried out or showed by example what he required of the disciples before he had any expectation of them to fulfill his commandments. Likewise, the leaders of the Church must do and teach the congregation what to do. They must be the first partakers. Oftentimes, church leaders preach a do as I say message and not a do as I do message. Ephesians 4:11-15 supports this concept of doing and then teaching:

"And he gave some, apostles; and some, prophets; and some, evangelists; and some, pastors and teachers; For the perfecting of the saints, for the work of the ministry, for the edifying of the body of Christ: Till we all come in the unity of the faith, and of the knowledge of the Son of God, unto a perfect man, unto the measure of the stature of the fullness of Christ: ...But speaking the truth in love, may grow up into him in all things, which is the head, even Christ:"

Teaching involves the concept of mentoring. A mentor is a person who advises or trains a younger colleague. It also encompasses guidance, emotional support, motivation, help and knowledge to a less experienced person. Most of us have heard the phrase, *"each one teach one"*. The Church has numerous ways in which it can exercise a mentoring program by following Jesus example. Jesus preached for three and a half years in the countryside of Israel. He handpicked twelve men, who he personally mentored during this period of time. And today, there are over 1.8 billion believers in the world as a result of Biblical mentoring.

It is often said that the most vulnerable people in society are the children and the elderly. Both groups can benefit from a mentoring program. Many children and seniors don't have an extended support system. The children are often left to their own devices with plenty of time on their hands without structure. Idle minds in the children can lead to experimenting with drugs, addiction to video games, gang involvement, depression, and even suicidal mindsets. Basic needs of the children and the elderly generally fall through the cracks and go unattended. The church can fill in these gaps by supplying the need. What Jesus began, we must continue. Let us look at some ways in which the pastor and every Christian can mentor others to continue to change the world for Jesus.

Community Outreach Programs

After School Program
After school programs are an excellent way to partner with

parents and schools to provide additional help for the children with their homework and social skill development. Children no matter what age love to interact with adults that are successful in areas that they have an interest. Therefore every skill set from the volunteers would be appreciated and greatly needed. At our church New Creation in Brooklyn, we have created an afterschool program with church volunteers ranging from retirees, young adults, teachers, mothers and men. They provide homework assistance, snacks, a listening ear or supervision for games or movies. Some times they pray with the children, play Bible trivia games, teach them a song or give them pointers in the sports they are interested in. Most importantly they give themselves to the children in whatever way is needed for that day.

Senior Outreach

Elderly people are very prone to depression. Often times, no one visits them or spend quality time with them. Nursing homes and senior facilities often will welcome volunteers to come in and minister to the seniors. Basic chores of helping them to tidy up their room, take a walk outside or to the community room, reading mail or the Bible, sharing a meal together, accompanying them to a medical appointment and playing a board game would be greatly appreciated.

Food Pantry

Jesus demonstrated the need to feed hungry people numerous times in his ministry. Having sufficient and basic food is a requirement for all people. It is the means by which we are able to gain good nutrition for our bodies and do the work of God. Whether it was the 4,000 (see Mark 8:1-9) or the 5,000 (see Luke 9:12-17), Jesus did not take a roll call of why the people did not have their own food. He simply had compassion on the people and provided for them out of the resources that were available to him. A food pantry is not just for the homeless as some would think, it is for all who are hungry and need to stretch whatever finances they have. It is for the struggling single mother, the elderly person on a pension, the unemployed or the person who is recovering from a recent surgery or hospitalization. This is a wonderful opportunity to teach others of God's love and Jesus sacrifices. Providing a Thanksgiving basket once a year is not enough time to teach or birth another disciple. Any kind of outreach food ministry must be consistent in order for it to impact the givers and those receiving the food.

Coat Drive

I live in New York and it can get very cold during the winter months, so having a proper winter coat is a necessity. I have seen many children only wearing a lightweight hoody during twenty-degree weather shivering and yet pretending to be warm. Jesus made it clear that we have a responsibility to clothe those that are naked or have insufficient garments. He further stated,

> *"Inasmuch as ye have done it unto one of the least of these my brethren, ye have done it unto me"* (see Matthew 25:35-40).

There are a variety of ways to get coats to donate to those who have none. Many local stores are willing to partner with the church and donate coats especially at the end of the winter season. These can be stored for the upcoming winter season. Local dry cleaners will also donate or sell coats inexpensively that have not been picked up by the owner. Leaders in the congregation can donate a fairly new coat or can sacrifice and purchase a new one for a child or anyone else who is in need. As the leaders demonstrate the "to do and teach" principle others will follow them. Wonderful lessons can be taught to the congregation as they learn to take up their cross, deny self and follow Jesus in their coat drive participation.

Partnering With The School

Many parents have a misconception of what the schools job is in the life of their child. Some believe it is the responsibility of the school to not only educate the child but also to discipline, babysit, mentor, prepare meals and nurture social skills. Christian parents ought to be an example of ones who aid the educational system with their child rather than fault them. Go into the world includes going into the school system. The Parent Teachers Association (PTA) is a partnership between parents and educators to enhance student learning and enrich the lives of the student within the school. It also serves as a forum for parents to obtain knowledge and voice their concerns about what is happening in their child's school. Joining the PTA is a first step to bring the presence of the Lord into the learning process. This partnership allows parents to play a more effective role in encouraging their child to excel and do great exploits for the Lord. The educators would also welcome volunteers to assist them in the many duties that are daily before them.

Personal Mentoring

I have personally encouraged and made provisions for our congregation to play a consistent role in the mentorship process as we heed to fulfill the Great Commission. This is our mission statement at New Creation Christian Church:

"Our goal is to reach those men and women, boys and girls that have been broken through life's unfortunate circumstances, and that through the love and word of Christ, we will nurture them into a New Creation. As a Body of Believers we vow to exalt the Lord, edify the believers, evangelize the lost and enhance our community".

As a result of our commitment to our mission statement, we've created various outreach ministries to engage the community and members of our congregation. Every Saturday between the hours of 12-2pm, our food pantry is open to help feed our community.

Our after school homework center is available Monday

through Friday from 3-7pm to partner with parents and the school to make our children successful members of society. We've further developed a Big Brother/Big Sisters Mentorship Program, Leap 4 Faith Basketball Tournament, and a High School Diploma program. Each program is undergirded with prayer and a willingness to teach with a deliberate intent to make disciples. Our model is simple; just do what Jesus would do to meet the need as it is presented to us. Every church regardless of its size can do as Jesus has done.

CHAPTER 5

Empty Vessels

"And the earth was without form, and void.." (Genesis 1:2).

When God recognized that the earth he created was without form and was void or empty, he did something miraculous about it. He began his awesome work of speaking into existence those things he desired in the earth. As I began to examine the attributes of God, the character of God and the behavior of God, I find that God likes filling things. Throughout the first chapter of Genesis, we see a long list of the things that God filled. He filled the firmament of heaven with the sun, the moon, the stars and the planets. He filled the waters with fish and whales. He filled the open firmament of heaven with birds. He filled the earth with trees, plants, beasts and cattle. His greatest filling was when he created man and filled him with himself (see Genesis 1:1-27, 2:7).

God's ultimate desire and plan for mankind is that each person would consistently remain filled with his Spirit. Unfortunately the disobedience of men, the cares of this world, the subtleness of Satan, and the laziness of men has caused many of God's children to be empty vessels who cannot fulfilling their divine destiny. God considers us empty vessels when we do not have his Holy Spirit in us. The room or space that should be filled by Holy Spirit is filled with the devil and his influence. Therefore there is no presence of the Lord and no concern for the state or condition of the blind.

Why Are Our Vessels Empty?

> *"O foolish Galatians, who hath bewitched you, that ye should not obey the truth, before whose eyes Jesus Christ hath been evidently set forth, crucified among you? Are ye so foolish? having begun in the Spirit, are ye now made perfect by the flesh"* **(see Galatians 3:1,3)?**

The Apostle Paul shares with the church at Galatia that when they don't obey the truth it is as if they were being controlled by sorcery. He warns them that they must continue to fix their eyes on Christ and resist the flesh in order to maintain a right relationship with him. Likewise, when we lean to our own understanding and don't obey God's word we place our self on the path to become an empty vessel.

Let us look into the Holy Scripture at the life of Samson and the Prodigal Son and see why their vessel became empty.

Empty Vessels

In the Book of Judges we learn about Samson. He was prepared by God as a Nazarite from birth to deliver Israel. He was born to deliver God's people who had been crying to God to send a judge that would deliver them from the Philistine bondage. In his many victories against the Philistines, he became prideful, boastful, began to lean to his own understanding and flirted with ungodly things and people like Delilah. He rejected his godly parents wisdom, allowed lust to entice him, defiled himself, used his power/skill wrongfully and placed confidence in himself and his own ability. Samson demonstrates how terrible it was and is to have amnesia (loss of memory) when it comes to putting God first. He was filled with the Spirit of God from the womb because God heard the cry of the oppressed. During his youth he had sight to see the need of those who had been crying out to God for help. By the end of his life his continual sin caused God to depart from him (see Judges 16:20) and he became an empty vessel. Samson had forgotten that he was God's man and not his own. The enemies of God made him blind and subject to ridicule. All that remained was a repentant man who only wanted to have enough mercy to do one last act of destroying God's enemies with the sacrifice of his own life. Whenever we follow in Samson's footstep and fail to make God our priority, we too will become empty vessels.

In Luke chapter 15, the Apostle Luke introduces us to the prodigal or empty son. This was a young man that seemed to have the right family, comforts, and blessings that others would desire and yet he was not satisfied. This young man boldly told his father to give him his inheritance, though his father was alive. Inheritances are generally dispersed between siblings when the parent dies. Not only did he hear an evil voice whispering in his ear, he also chose to follow it rather than cast down those wicked thoughts. He cared not for the cry of his elder brother or his father's desire for him to stay and help them. His selfishness, greed, impatience, immaturity and lack of discernment delivered him into a far country. After he had spent all that he had, he began to be in want. The only work he could find was that of feeding the swine. He was so hungry that he desired the pig's food. No one showed him compassion. Empty vessels are characterized by an absence of content. What should be inside is noticeably missing. In his need and desperation for food, he began to realize that everything was better in his father's house where Holy Spirit was allowed to be in control.

In the suffering of Samson and the Prodigal Son, they learned that the wages of sin is spiritual death. Sin will cause a separation between God and us. No matter how small we think a sin to be, it will always leave us empty.

Again, God does not like empty things. Even as he filled everything that was empty in Genesis chapter one, he is still seeking to fill men with himself. Even the Apostles admonished us to be filled with the Spirit. When the Bible speaks of being filled with the Holy Spirit, it speaks of being under the influence of the Holy Spirit, it means to be intoxicated or totally controlled by Holy Spirit. We must be filled with the Spirit in order to hear the cry of the blind and respond to it. Otherwise our sin will leave us empty and we will be of no service to God or anyone else.

CRY OF THE BLIND

CHAPTER 6

Be Filled With The Spirit

In spite of us, God continually uses every opportunity to refill men. Let us look at the example of what happened on the day of Pentecost.

> *"And when the day of Pentecost was fully come, they were all with one accord in one place. And suddenly there came a sound from heaven as of a rushing mighty wind, and it filled all the house where they were sitting. And there appeared unto them cloven tongues like as of fire, and it sat upon each of them. And they were all filled with the Holy Ghost, and began to speak with other tongues, as the Spirit gave them utterance" (Acts Chapter 2:1- 4).*

CRY OF THE BLIND

First God filled the house or the physical place in which they were gathered, and then he filled all of those who were in the house with his Spirit. He also filled their bellies with living waters and their mouths with power and authority to rightly divide the word.

The Lord knew that being filled with His Spirit was the only way that his followers could fulfill his divine mandate of going into all the earth to make disciples of men.

This Christian walk was not to be a selfish or a self-fulfilling journey. It is a discipleship-making journey.

Throughout the Book of Acts, we witness the apostles and disciples being refilled over and over again. If the apostles needed to be refilled, it should be an indication that we also need to be refilled. Our vessels will leak if we are doing the work of the Lord and become empty when we are fulfilling our own agenda. So in either case, we need to be refilled.

Acts 4:8 "Then Peter, filled with the Holy Ghost, said unto them, Ye rulers of the people, and elders of Israel, If we this day be examined if the good deed done to the impotent man, by what means he is made whole; Be it known unto you all, and to all the people of Israel, that by the name of Jesus Christ of Nazareth... this man stand here before you whole".

Acts 4:31 "And when they had prayed, the place was shaken where they were assembled together; and they were filled with the Holy Ghost, and they spake the word of God with boldness."

Acts 9:17 "And Ananias went his way, and entered into the house; and putting his hands on him said, Brother Saul, the Lord, even Jesus, that appeared unto thee in the way as thou camest, hath sent me, that thou mightiest receive thy sight, and be filled with the Holy Ghost".

Jesus shares the need to win souls by teaching the parable of the great supper to his disciples. The key verse was the following,

"And the lord said unto the servant, Go out into the highways and hedges, and compel them to come in, that my house may be filled" (Luke 14: 23).

God reminded me that the church must be set in order. We have drifted away from allowing Holy Spirit to fill us. Many people want to be used in God's house without having a personal relationship with him. When there is a return to prayer services and Bible study the leaders will be equipped to function in God's house. I am convinced that secondary leaders, department heads, ushers and ministry of helps volunteers have to be filled with Holy Spirit in order to do the work of the evangelist. It is when we are filled with Holy Spirit that rivers of living waters will flow out of our belly. We will hear the cry of the blind and know what we are to do to bring about healing.

How To Refill Your Vessel:

"If my people, which are called by my name, shall

humble themselves, and pray, and seek my face, and turn from their wicked ways; then will I hear from heaven, and will forgive their sin, and will heal their land" (2 Chronicles 7:14).

The best way to refill our vessel is summed up in 2 Chronicles 7:14. Through humility, prayer, seeking God's face and repentance our empty vessels will be refilled. When we return to God his way, He will turn those stagnant situations around and refill us for his work.

Humility is not something that we all run to embrace. Most of us don't want to seem weak or of little importance in the sight of others. It is often difficult to be meek, modest, unassertive or submissive in a world that pressures us to be some special one. The scripture says that Jesus humbled himself and became obedient unto death (see Philippians 2:8). We too must follow in Jesus footstep and demonstrate by our actions that we are humbling our self in the sight of God. We need to go back to serving Christ by serving others. Those areas of service where we are not out front before people will be a great place to begin. We can volunteer to be part of the cleaning ministry, hospitality, audio, or the children ministry at our church.

Prayer is almost null and void in the life of some who profess to be Christians. When we first got saved, we couldn't wait for an opportunity to talk with God. We were sometimes the first one in a prayer meeting and now we find all kinds of excuses as to why we can't gather with the saints to make our request known to God. The apostles demonstrated a return to prayer each time God used them to do some great exploit. They didn't take it for granted but demonstrated a dependency on seeking instructions from the Master. They wanted to be filled with God's wisdom, discernment and power therefore they prayed.

The prophet Jeremiah reminds us,

> *"And ye shall seek me, and find me, when ye shall search for me with all your heart. And I will be found of you, saith the Lord" (Jeremiah 29:13-14):*

Seeking the Lord, means to earnestly and diligently look for God's presence and not just material blessings. When we are conscious of God's presence we will yield our self to his service. Where he leads we will follow.

"Lord I'm sorry" and "Lord I'm wrong" is two of the hardest things for us to say. Only when we are willing to repent and turn from our sin can the Lord Jesus forgive us. Until we repent we will not be refreshed, revived, or renewed. Holy Spirit will not come to live in a dirty, overstuffed and uninviting house. Light and dark cannot dwell together. Jesus already stated that we are the light of the world, yet unrepentant sin in our lives has darkened us to resemble the world. God desires that none of us would perish and experience eternal damnation. Therefore, he is still beckoning us make an about face and stop sinning.

CRY OF THE BLIND

We are not witnessing or seeing more unbelievers become converted to Christianity because we have been deceived to believe that we are filled with the Spirit and are not.

In order to be refilled, the things that we've become slacked in, the things we discarded and began to treat as if it had no value are going to be the very things we must pick up, dust off and do. Go back and pick up prayer, Bible reading and Bible study, attending Sunday school class, fellowshipping with the saints, testifying of God's goodness and inviting people to church. These are not the prerequisite for the pastor. These are for all Christians that would desire to be filled and remain filled. God has said in the Holy Scripture that once we humble our self, pray, seek his face and turn from our wicked ways he would heal or refill our empty vessels. God cannot lie. Our vessel will be refilled when we obey his commandment.

CHAPTER 7

Return To The Mission

"The harvest truly is plenteous, but the laborers are few;" Matthew 9:37

God has been calling his people from the beginning of time and he is still calling us today to the mission field. The mission field is not some third world country, it is right inside and outside of your doors. The need still exists for the harvest to be gathered. The problem is not with the harvest but with the laborers. Let us look at three pillars in the Holy Scriptures that God called to his mission of gathering the harvest.

> *"And the Lord God called unto Adam, and said unto him, Where art thou?" (Genesis 3:9).*

> *"And the Lord called yet again, Samuel" (1 Samuel 3:6).*

> *"And he fell to the earth, and heard a voice saying unto him, Saul, Saul, why persecutes thou me? (Acts 9:4).*

The calling of Adam, Samuel & Saul of Tarsus was much more than what meets the eye. They weren't being called to go to a physical place. They were being called to return to the place of their original calling to occupy, subdue and have authority over all that is in the earth. Each one of these men was called to make an impression on the people and culture about them.

The church and the people of God must leave an impression on this world. An impression is a strong effect or influence produced on the intellect, feeling, or the conscience of an individual. The root word press means to act upon with steadily applied weight or force in a certain direction or into a certain position. It also has the underlying meaning of compressing or squeezing with the end result to alter in shape or size. So, it is our responsibility not to be pressured, but to apply pressure to situations or things to bring about a change. We can also say that we are to make an imprint or a mark that would identify us by a name or title. It has always been and still is God's will for the man that he created to leave an impression on the earth. The world is not impressed with the church today because the church has not left an imprint on the world. We have not applied our weight upon the world. We have become too passive, laid back and at ease in Zion. We need to go back to the basics of doing what God called us to do. Many preachers are weak and compromising. Therefore, the gospel they preach is weak, unimpressive and ineffective. So, instead of the world following the church, the church is now following the world. There is only one star in the world and in the church, his name is Jesus Christ, the Bright and Morning Star. Jesus called those who are a part of his church, the light of the world. He does not call the world the light of the church. It is our duty to let our light shine before men, that they may see our good works, and give glory to our Father (see Matthew 5:16).

Sometimes the calling of the world seems louder than the calling of God and this causes some people to struggle.

The word compromise means a middle way between two extremes. It can be defined as making accommodations in which both sides make concessions. In other words some people are stuck in the middle of here and there. This is the condition Israel found itself when Joshua admonished them,

> *"And if it seem evil unto you to serve the LORD, choose you this day whom ye will serve; whether the gods which your fathers served that were on the other side of the flood, or the gods of the Amorites, in whose land ye dwell: but as for me and my house, we will serve the LORD"* (Joshua 24:15).

There are only two ways that we can respond to God's call.

CRY OF THE BLIND

Either we say yes to his will or we say no. Adam responded to the call by hiding himself and making excuses. This clearly was the same as saying no, I will not return to the mission of subduing the land and taking authority over it. As a result of Adam making excuses, he lost his authority over his wife, the animals and the very earth itself. He would never regain control again in this life. What he should have controlled was now controlling him. Adam no doubt felt ashamed. He could not seem to get pass his failure with the serpent therefore he blocked his destiny. He developed a feeling of shame, and guilt, with feelings of inferiority, inadequacy, remorse and embarrassment. Satan wasn't satisfied with the fall in the Garden; he was still at work looking for ways to embarrass the man of God.

We too fail to realize that God uses the unfortunate situations in our life to place us on the right road of divine destiny. Though a good man falls seven times, God will still help him to get up if his answer is yes to the call. Samuel and Saul of Tarsus's answer was yes. Samuel answered the Lord in the affirmative when he responded, ***"Here am I"*** and Saul of Tarsus responded with these words, ***"Lord what will you have me to do?"*** Samuel fulfilled his divine destiny to become one of the greatest prophets that Israel witnessed by yielding to God's will. Saul of Tarsus fulfilled his destiny becoming known to the world as the Apostle Paul who wrote Romans and thirteen other epistles in the New Testament all because he looked to Jesus and not his pass failures.

In order to return to the mission, we must follow in the footsteps of the children of Israel and choose to serve and obey the Lord (see Joshua 24:21-24). Along with making God our choice, we must have a made up mind to immediately respond not like Adam but like Samuel and Saul of Tarsus. God is not going to go against your volition (your will).
Though he wanted Adam to rule the earth, he was not going to force anything on him. Likewise, if you and I say no to the Lord, he will not force us to reap the blessings of obedience. Scripture is very clear that God is still willing to recommission us just like he did Jonah, if we would repent and return to the mission God will use us.

"Remember therefore from whence thou art fallen, and repent, and do the first works; or else I will come unto thee quickly, and will remove thy candlestick out of his place, except thou repent" (Revelations 2:5).

God said go back and do your first work over, let's go back and evangelize the way God said to do it.

CRY OF THE BLIND

CHAPTER 8

I'm Not Ashamed Of The Gospel

"For I am not ashamed of the gospel of Christ: for it is the power of God unto salvation to every one that believeth; to the Jew first, and also to the Greek" (Romans 1:16)

There are many so-called Christians that are hiding in the closet. Only the clothes and shoes in the closet know that they are Christians. Neighbors, co-workers and even family members don't know or see any evidence of their Christianity. Because they fear what men will say or do to them, they keep quiet and hide their lights under a bushel. Some want the praise or approval of men more than the rewards of obedience to their creator.

Peter is an example of a professing disciple who became ashamed of the Messiah when Judas betrayed Christ (see Matthew 26:69-75). Peter was so filled with shame that he could not acknowledge his alliance with Jesus and thereby denied him three times. His level of embarrassment was so great he did not want anyone to put him as an acquaintance of Jesus.

To further say he was a disciple of someone who at the time looked like they had no power or authority to preserve their own life was too much for him. The mere thought that he could face the same punishment as Jesus caused him to be unwilling to walk near him. Peter totally forgot that out of his own mouth he spoke that Jesus was the Son of God. He even told Jesus that he would die with him. Yet now when the rubber is meeting the road, Peter out of shame and embarrassment distance himself from Jesus the Savior of the world.

Let us looking into the word of God concerning what it teaches about being ashamed.

> *"For I am not ashamed of the gospel of Christ: for it is the power of God unto salvation to everyone that believeth; to the Jew first, and also to the Greek" (Romans 1:16).*

> *"For the scripture saith, whosoever believeth on him*

shall not be ashamed. For there is no difference between the Jew and the Greek: for the same Lord over all is rich unto all that call upon him. For whosoever shall call upon the name of the Lord shall be saved" (Romans 10:11-13).

"For God hath not given us the spirit of fear; but of power, and of love, and of a sound mind. Be not thou therefore ashamed of the testimony of our Lord, nor of me his prisoner: but be thou partaker of the afflictions of the gospel according to the power of God; Who hath saved us, and called us with an holy calling, not according to our works, but according to his own purpose and grace, which was given us in Christ Jesus before the world began" (2 Timothy 1:7-9),

"And hope maketh not ashamed; because the love of God is shed abroad in our hearts by the Holy Ghost which is given unto us." Romans 5:5

"For if I have boasted any thing to him of you, I am not ashamed; but as we spake all things to you in truth, even so our boasting, which I made before Titus, is found a truth" (2 Corinthians 7:14).

"For the which cause I also suffer these things: nevertheless I am not ashamed: for I know whom I have believed, and am persuaded that he is able to keep that which I have committed unto him against that day" (2 Timothy 1:12).

"The Lord give mercy unto the house of Onesiphorus; for he oft refreshed me, and was not ashamed of my chain" (2 Timothy 1:16):

> *"Study to shew thyself approved unto God, a workman that needeth not to be ashamed, rightly dividing the word of truth"* (2 Timothy 2:15).

> *"Yet if any man suffer as a Christian, let him not be ashamed; but let him glorify God on this behalf"* (1 Peter 4:16).

As we have set our eyes on the scriptures above, we find that it is clear that we should not be ashamed of the Good News or our Savior. The final conclusion is that the scriptures must be the final authority in how we address thoughts and feelings of shame. We should not be ashamed of Christ or embarrassed of the work he has assigned us to carry out. Those who are ashamed of the gospel cannot help the Blind Bartimaeus's of the world.

We are called to evangelize or preach the gospel with the ultimate goal of converting someone to Christianity. The Bible says,

> *"But ye shall receive power, after that the Holy Ghost is come upon you: and ye shall be witnesses, unto me both in Jerusalem, and in all Judaea, and in Samaria, and unto the uttermost part of the earth"* (Acts 1:8).

It is our responsibility, to help God reach the lost and to help the blind find what they are looking for. The hour has come, and now is, that Christians must take a stand and set their face as flint and share the Good News of salvation with boldness. Being ashamed is not an option when people are dying around us and going to hell.

CHAPTER 9

Search For The Lost

"for this thy brother was dead, and is alive again; and was lost, and is found" (Luke 15:32b)

Luke chapter 15 contains three parables that speak about lost things and the need for the owner to find it. These parables deal with the lost sheep, the lost coin, and the lost son. The term lost and found can be associated with this text. These parables introduce the importance of sinners to Jesus. The text reveals the focus and tension (pressure, worry, conflict, strain) that is created in an attempt to find something that has been lost. Anyone who has ever lost anything can identify with this type of tension. For example when you lose your keys, can't find your glasses and can't find money that was just in your hand tension builds. Because of the tension that is created, an all points bulletin will be sent out to your entire family or those in your home. Your children will be on the hunt for those items, your spouse will begin to search pants pockets, brooms will be employed to sweep behind couches, flashlights will be utilized and no one will stop looking until someone retrieves the item. When the lost item is found, not only is the person who had misplaced it relieved, but also the whole search party is relieved that the missing items have been found.

Jesus spoke this parable to the disciples, saying,

"What man of you, having an hundred sheep, if he lose one of them, doth not leave the ninety and nine in the wilderness, and go after that which is lost, until he find it? And when he hath found it, he layeth it on his shoulders, rejoicing. And when he cometh home, he calleth together his friends and neighbours, saying unto them, Rejoice with me; for I have found my sheep which was lost. I say unto you, that likewise joy shall be in heaven over one sinner that repenteth, more than over ninety and nine just persons, which need no repentance" (Luke Chapter 15:3-7).

Jesus further continues to illustrate his point with this second parable of the lost coin.

"Either what woman having ten pieces of silver, if she lose one piece, doth not light a candle, and sweep the house, and seek diligently till she find it? And when she hath found it, she calleth her friends and her neighbours

together, saying, Rejoice with me; for I have found the piece which I had lost. Likewise, I say unto you, there is joy in the presence of the angels of God over one sinner that repenteth" (Luke 15:8).

Jesus began these series of parables with the subject of a lost animal, a lost coin and finally he speaks of the most important subject a lost person. This was deliberate and calculating. He wanted to drive the message home that a person created in the image of God was the most important thing that should be sought after, located and restored to the rightful owner. Here is what he shares with the disciples about the lost son.

"And he arose, and came to his father. But when he was yet a great way off, his father saw him, and had compassion, and ran, and fell on his neck, and kissed him. And the son said unto him, Father, I have sinned against heaven, and in thy sight, and am no more worthy to be called thy son. But the father said to his servants, Bring forth the best robe, and put it on him; and put a ring on his hand, and shoes on his feet: And bring hither the fatted calf, and kill it: and let us eat, and be merry: For this my son was dead, and is alive again; he was lost, and is found. And they began to be merry" (Luke 15:22-24).

The fact that Jesus was willing to die for the lost is an indication that lost people is important to God. We were brought with a price and are not our own. Jesus paid the price for each of us without asking for a discount. You were worth dying for. Once a person repents of their sin and receives the atoning work of Christ heaven rejoices over them. You have been restored to your rightful owner and are no more in the far country. If you know you were lost and have been found, take a moment and reflect on that wonderful miracle that was bestowed on you. If you are still lost in your sin, you do not have to remain that way anymore. The same way the lost son asked his Father to forgive him and allow him to return home is the same way you can ask Jesus to forgive you and receive you into his family. There will be a celebration party for you as well.

When we search for someone or something it means to carefully look for what may be hidden out of sight or lost. If the item or person is very important to us, we will get additional help. We will organize a search party or a group of people to look for the valuable pet/item/person that has been lost, but have not lost their value. Likewise, we are commissioned to look for the blind and search for them one by one. We should have been searching for Blind Bartimeaus and others like him who needed to be brought to Jesus. Even as it was important to God to send Jesus to look for us, we must develop the same mind that was in Christ and search high and low for others. The scriptures cannot be broken when we seek we will find the Blind Bartimeaus's.

CHAPTER 10

Use The Name Of Jesus

"If ye shall ask anything in my name, I will do it" (John 14:14).

Names were very significant in the Old Testament and the New Testament. Some names were given to communicate God's message to his people. The prophet Hosea was told to name his children Jezreel (I will avenge the blood of Jezreel upon the house of Jehu), Loruhamah (for I will no more have mercy upon the house of Israel), and Loammi (for ye are not my people, and I will not be your God) (see Hosea 1:3-9). Names were also given to demonstrate an affiliation with God. Such was the case in Genesis 32:28 concerning Jacob.

The Lord changed his name from Jacob to Israel (for a prince has thou power with God and with men, and has prevailed). We also see similar name changes in the New Testament involving Simon Barjona who was renamed Peter (see Matthew 16:17-18) and Saul of Tarsus who we now know as the Apostle Paul (see Acts 13:9). In light of the significance of a name, Jesus told us over and over again to use his name whenever we are requesting anything from the Father.

Jesus name means the one who has power to deliver, rescue or bring salvation to his people.

> *"For whosoever shall call upon the name of the Lord shall be saved" (Romans 10:13).*

We sometimes are like many unbelievers, including alcoholics, drug users, thieves and adulterers, who have heard the name of Jesus, but don't know the power that's in his name. Blind Bartimaeus seemed to have been more knowledgeable about the power that was in the name of Jesus than the scribes and Pharisees who sought to deny him access to Jesus. Though he could not see, he was blessed because he knew what name was associated with the power that could heal him.

> *"Woe unto you, scribes and Pharisees, hypocrites! for ye pay tithe of mint and anise and cummin, and have omitted the weightier matters of the law, judgment, mercy, and faith: these ought ye to have done, and not to leave the other undone" (Matthew 23:23).*

Jesus called the scribes and the Pharisees out for being a stumbling block to those like Blind Bartimaeus who was seeking the Lord. The scribes and Pharisees were very knowledgeable about the significance of names and what they represented; yet in their own jealously they pretended deaf to Bartimaeus's cry for Jesus. They would have been happier if the blind man had called their name instead of Jesus. Sometimes we want people to call our name rather than the name of Jesus. There really is only one name that can save; it's not my name or your name. Only the name of Jesus can save.

Like the scribes and Pharisees, we often choose to discard the teachings of Jesus that we have no intention of observing. They found it easy to embrace the teaching on tithing, giving a freewill offering to the church and even church service attendance, however they did not freely embrace the teachings on love, mercy or faith. Being learned men, they should have been able to digest strong meat, yet they still had need of drinking milk (see Hebrews 5:12).

Blind Bartimeaus was not a learned man, but he could understand the teaching on mercy (compassion, kindness, pity, and generosity) because he needed mercy.

"And he cried, saying, Jesus, thou son of David, have mercy on me" (Luke 18:38).

He further demonstrated his understanding of mercy by asking for it.

"And he said Lord, that I may receive my sight" (Luke 18:41).

Blind Bartimaeus was able to equate the name of Jesus of Nazareth with the son of David.

CRY OF THE BLIND

"And he cried, saying, Jesus, thou son of David," (Luke 18:38).

It was evident that the Holy Spirit must have revealed to him that Jesus was the one the prophet's spoke about that would heal, deliver and rule over nations. He didn't just cry to Jesus to exercise his vocal cords. He ascribed power and ability to the name of Jesus. He expected that this Jesus could do for him what no man or physician could have done for him.

Sometimes when we don't want to change our actions, we reject those teachings that would demand an immediate change. Such was the case for the scribes and the Pharisees. Though they followed Jesus closely, they did not embrace what he taught about love and mercy. Neither did they ascribe any authority in his name though he was God in the flesh.

The Israelites made it a point of their duty to teach the scriptures to their children. They were fully persuaded that they must preserve the words of God to Moses and the prophets with the next generation. Perhaps the father of Blind Bartimaeus had taught him the sacred scriptures and therefore he knew that a Savior would come. Knowing that the word and name of the Lord endured forever, he had good reason to call on Jesus. Even though he only had the Old Testament teachings, Bartimaeus believed the word of God.

Here is what the scriptures in the Old and New Testament teach us about the name of the Lord Jesus Christ and why we should call or ask him for the things we need.

"..then began men too call upon the name of the Lord" (Genesis 4:26).

"Then called I upon the name of the Lord; O Lord, I beseech thee, deliver my soul" (Psalm 116:4).

"Our help is in the name of the Lord, who made heaven and earth" (Psalm 124:8).

"..whosoever shall call on the name of the Lord shall be delivered" (Joel 2:32):

"And it shall come to pass, that whosoever shall call on the name of the Lord shall be saved" (Acts 2:21).

"And whatsoever ye shall ask in my name, that will I do, that the Father may be glorified in the Son. If ye shall ask anything in my name, I will do it" (John 14:13-14).

"Whatsoever ye shall ask the Father in my name, he will give it you" (John 16:23).

"At that day ye shall ask in my name: and I say not unto you, that I will pray the Father for you" (John 16:26):

"..that whatsoever ye shall ask of the Father in my name, he may give it you" (John 15:16).

"For whosoever shall call upon the name of the Lord shall be saved" (Romans 10:13).

CRY OF THE BLIND

The scriptures above confirm that using the name of Jesus is the only way to guarantee that whatsoever we ask according to God's will it shall be done for us. Let us boldly ask for the blind (see Psalm 2:8) in Jesus name and gather the harvest.

Chapter 11

Evangelize The Blind

"Preach the word; be instant in season, out of season; reprove, rebuke, exhort with all longsuffering and doctrine" (2 Timothy 4:2).

The scribes and Pharisees were called to do the work of teaching the scriptures to the people. They were to evangelize the sinner and yet they failed Blind Bartimaeus. Every professing Christian is called to do the work of the evangelist. It is our duty and responsibility to preach the gospel with the goal of converting someone to Christianity.

CRY OF THE BLIND

Jesus came to seek and save those who were lost. If we are going to be like Jesus, we must evangelize the lost.

Luke records Jesus last spoken words concerning evangelism to the disciples in the Book of Acts.

> *"But, ye shall receive power, after that the Holy Ghost is come upon you: and ye shall be witnesses unto me both in Jerusalem, and in all Judaea, and in Samaria, and unto the uttermost part of the earth" (Acts 1:8).*

In this verse of scripture, the word witnesses refer to role and work of the evangelist.

The Apostle Paul builds upon what Jesus taught the disciples by clearly making known the various purpose and roles of ministry leaders.

> *"And he gave some, apostles; and some, prophets; and some, evangelists; and some, pastors and teachers; For the perfecting of the saints, for the work of the ministry, for the edifying of the body of Christ: Till we all come in the unity of the faith, and of the knowledge of the Son of God, unto a perfect man, unto the measure of the stature of the fullness of Christ" (Ephesians 4:11-13):*

In the above scriptures, we see the importance of the work of the evangelist. The evangelist is placed in the middle of all the other ministry leaders. It can be said that the apostles govern, the prophet's guide, the evangelists gather, and the pastors and teachers lay the foundation. Without the evangelist, the apostle has no one to govern, the prophet has no one to guide, and the pastor and teacher have no one to build a foundation in. Evangelism in essence is truly the heartbeat of ministry. Without the blind, lost and infirmed coming into the church there will be no one to minister to.

The Apostle Paul encourages the young pastor Timothy to evangelize. He said,

"But watch thou in all things, endure afflictions, do the work of an evangelist, make full proof of thy ministry" (2 Timothy 4:5).

The Apostle Paul shared with Timothy the need and necessity to fully perform all the duties of his ministry, which also included evangelizing the blind.

Throughout the Gospels, we learn that it was always Jesus custom to pray. It was his practice of communing with the Father that always enabled him to be at the right place at the right time to fulfill his ministry. The Apostle John shares with us in the fourth chapter of the book that bears his name, how Jesus evangelized the Samaritan woman at the well. He traveled out of his way, asked her to give him a drink of water, took away all prejudicial behavior, revealed her marital past, preached the Good News to her and brought deliverance in her life. The woman became so excited about what she heard and experienced that she ran into the city and evangelized her people. She cried out to them,

"Come see a man that told me everything that I have ever done: is not this the Christ? (John 4:29)"

When we pray we will be directed to the people who God is already drawing. Their heart will also be prepared to receive the engrafted word of truth.

Before Jesus ascended to the Father, he gave his disciples a simple command.

CRY OF THE BLIND

"Go ye therefore, and teach all nations, baptizing them in the name of the Father, and of the Son, and of the Holy Ghost: Teaching them to observe all things whatsoever I have commanded you: and, lo, I am with you always, even unto the end of the world" (Matthew 28:19-20).

This is the same command for us as well. The cry of the blind is louder today than it was yesterday. Let us respond to the cry of the blind and go and do the greater works Jesus spoke about.

The Conclusion

"I the LORD have called thee in righteousness, and will hold thine hand, and will keep thee, and give thee for a covenant of the people, for a light of the Gentiles; To open the blind eyes, to bring out the prisoners from the prison, and them that sit in darkness out of the prison house. And I will bring the blind by a way that they knew not; I will lead them in paths that they have not known: I will make darkness light before them, and crooked things straight. These things will I do unto them, and not forsake them" (Isaiah 42:6).

As the Lord has spoken to the prophet Isaiah concerning the nation of Israel, He spoke to me concerning The Cry Of The Blind. To the best of my ability I have endeavored to make the vision plain. I have written the things that God has impressed on my heart. I once was blind and God caused others to hear my cry and come to my rescue. Will you not join me and do the same for someone else?

I pray that this book will inspire you to go and do what you where created to do. To win the heart and minds of those who sit in darkness. So, mount up and go EVANGELIZE THE BLIND. If this book has enlightened, quickened and stirred you on the inside regarding evangelism, then share it with someone else. God is encouraging us to fulfill his commission to go into all the earth, preach the Good News, rescue the blind and make disciples of men.

CRY OF THE BLIND

About The Author

Bishop Wesley V. Knight was born and raised in Brooklyn, New York. He is the founder and senior pastor of New Creation Christian Church in Brooklyn, New York.

In 2004, by the leading of the Lord, He founded the New Creation Outreach Center which encompasses children and youth ministries (toy drive, leap of faith basketball tournament, mentoring program and after-school program), men and women ministries, food pantry, which currently feed 180 families per week.

He has received various leadership awards for his service to his community. He works faithfully with the local precinct and community clergy board.

He is Founder and General Overseer for the New York City CCFM Leadership Alliance a fellowship of over 22 churches throughout New York & Baltimore.

He is in the *"making people lives better business"*.

Bishop Knight has studied to show himself approve unto God by obtaining a Bachelor's Degree in Theological Studies as well as receiving two Honorary Doctoral Degrees in his effort to be a workman that need not be ashamed.

He has two music projects to his credit "Live in New York" and "In Your Presence".

He is currently the Fire Safety Director for Memorial Sloan Kettering Cancer Center in New York City.

He and his wife Adriene have been married since March 1994 and together have two daughters, Camille and Christina.

Bishop Knight also has an older daughter, Kenyetta and a grandson, Jamel.

He is a faithful servant, husband, father, mentor, song writer, and student of the Word.

Contact the Author

Wesley V. Knight
1534 Broadway
Brooklyn, NY 11221

Phone: 917-554-7390

web: www.newccchurch.org

Email: pastorw.knight@aol.com

Bishop Knight is available to any church or group who wishes to have him come and minister for a conference, seminar or discussion, etc.

contact: Elder Nicole Johnson
Executive Administrator
nicolegj@aol.com

CRY OF THE BLIND

Additional Resources From Bishop Knight
Contact church for information on obtaining this and other resources.

CRY OF THE BLIND

GOD'S LIFE
PUBLISHING

God's Life Publishing is a ministry of God's Life Christian Church, and is dedicated to making resources available to the Body of Christ in the form of printed publications and e-books.

All resources has been reviewed for its spiritual edification content before we publish them for the Body of Christ.

HAWAII
5369 Edgewater Dr.
Ewa Beach, Hawaii 96076
Phone: 973 986-5407

For distributor, dealers, store locations or ordering information:
call or send an email to:
godlife@aol.com

godslifepublishing.org

CRY OF THE BLIND

www.ingramcontent.com/pod-product-compliance
Lightning Source LLC
Chambersburg PA
CBHW050444010526
44118CB00013B/1667